E 432 .B44

Bell, Carl Irving, 1912-

They knew Franklin Pierce
(and others thought they

DATE DUE

APR 20 '93			
OCT 0 1 1997			
DEC 1 7 1999			

THEY KNEW FRANKLIN PIERCE

They Knew

FRANKLIN PIERCE

(And Others Thought They Did)

By Carl Irving Bell

A sampling of opinions about

the 14th U.S. President drawn

from his contemporaries

April Hill Publishers, Springfield, Vermont

Printed in the United States of America by
Clifford-Nicol, Inc.
Plymouth, New Hampshire

To Phyllis

Preface

There have been many misunderstood men in public life but few Presidents besides Franklin Pierce who had such adulation at the start of the term and so much criticism when his administration ended. Some historians have claimed that he took the helm without knowing how to guide the ship of state. Others give the impression that he ordered a course which would beach the vessel on the shoals.

What is often forgotten is that there were powerful forces heading towards a confrontation and that Pierce prevented a North-South clash from taking place, though there was territorial strife. This compilation is not intended to defend the 14th President of the United States, nor to give him undue praise, but to present a cross-section of views prevailing in the latter half of the nineteenth century.

Most of the writers represented lived through the Pierce administration, and a number of the authors knew the President personally. Because Republicans predominated in politics with the election of Abraham Lincoln, many observers after 1860 felt an obligation to discredit the preceding Democratic administrations.

Since Franklin Pierce failed to participate in the Civil War, some former friends became detractors. Historians echoed the North's attitude by disregarding Pierce's accomplishments and pinning a label on his career that was hardly complimentary and scarcely accurate.

To bring together varying views by his contemporaries, this book is presented, without apology for omitting many writers who might well have been included if space permitted. A few authors, such as Nathaniel Hawthorne, have been left out because their work is either still in print or still well known. We have included more obscure comments on Franklin Pierce, despite the fact that we consider the

Hawthorne-Pierce relation one of the most fascinating friendships in American history.

We hope that the assembling of opinions and observations will interest the general reader as we do not pretend this to be a scholarly work with footnotes and other impedimenta. We also trust we shall be excused for occasionally inserting our own conclusions from time to time when we have felt that it was proper for us to intrude.

- - Carl Irving Bell.

While Nathaniel Hawthorne wrote the official campaign biography of Franklin Pierce, a more political review of his life was published by leading Democrats under authorship of D.W. Bartlett. The hastily assembled work was printed by Derby & Miller in the summer or early fall of 1852.

This is one of the few "lives" of Pierce which support the claim that he attended Exeter Academy before going on to Bowdoin College. Between terms he taught school for three months in Hebron, Maine, and Bartlett tells a story that has no special significance except that it is an early example of how chance played a great part in his life.

Unable to solve an arithmetic problem, he paced the floor of his room in the home of fellow student Zenas Caldwell and finally noticed a door to an opening in the chimney. Idly unlatching the small door, he found a sheet of paper on which was written the problem and its answer.

There would be other instances of coincidence, luck and, of course, inopportune tragedy throughout his life.

When New Hampshire recognized his service in the Legislature by sending him to Congress as a Representative, it may have been expected that this able orator would take the floor upon many issues. On the contrary, his work was mostly in committees and daily attendance at sessions. Bartlett has this explanation: "There was never at any time any need of his resorting to . . . franking thousands of his speeches to his constituents . . . by making a violent ado about nothing, in Congress, for the purpose of preserving his name fresh in the memories of his political supporters and friends."

Bartlett quotes the Boston Post as saying that Pierce was

one of the most influential Senators: "Without seeking popularity as a debater, Mr. Pierce, in the quiet and untiring pursuit of public duty, and the conscientious discharge of private responsibility, has acquired a permanent reputation, which places him among the most useful and efficient public men in the country."

The editor of the New England Puritan, who knew Pierce at Bowdoin, likewise had a compliment: "A very frank, gentlemanly, unobtrusive man is he, strongly devoted to his political principles, kind and constant in his friendship."

"In many respects," Bartlett wrote, "Mr. Pierce resembles General Jackson. He has the same iron will, the same honesty of character, and the same strong sympathies for the masses. But he possesses certain qualities which were never Jackson's. General Pierce is a graceful, polished man. There are few public men in the country who have such a power to make friends as he; therefore, during his residence in Washington, he made a wide circle of warm personal friends." Daniel Webster was mentioned as one of them, even though it had been felt that Webster would have been the Whig opponent to the Democratic nominee for the Presidency.

Bartlett did reproduce a number of speeches which Pierce delivered before the House and then the Senate, from which he resigned because of Mrs. Pierce's health in Washington's swampy climate. The lure of the governorship or a seat in Polk's cabinet as Attorney General did not bring Pierce back into public life though he did agree to serve as District Attorney of New Hampshire as this position was compatible with his legal profession and did not take him out of the state.

"Frank Pierce has shunned the avenues to great distinction," Bartlett concludes, "has refused the most inviting and flattering offices of preferment, that he might live in the bosom of his family, at Concord."

Bartlett makes clear that when the Mexican War broke out, Pierce did not jump from private to brigadier general almost overnight. "Mr. Pierce was among the first to put down his name, as a private soldier. The company was raised in Concord, and Frank Pierce went through all the drill exercises, as a private. The Ten Regiment Bill was passed by Congress, and the President tendered to him the appointment of Colonel of the Ninth, which appointment he accepted. When the law for the organization of the new ten regiments was passed, President Polk appointed Mr. Pierce Brigadier-General."

Many testimonials are given as to Pierce's bravery during the Mexican War, particularly a determination to fight on despite painful injuries. The author, and his apparent backers, were already aware that the opposition was charging Pierce with cowardice and with preventing Catholics from holding office in New Hampshire. Both claims were easily refuted by proving that the exact opposite was true.

Of Pierce's legal career following the Mexican War, Bartlett reports that "he never yet made a poor speech, and succeeds best with but little preparation - - upon the spur of the moment." This conclusion may be exaggerated but many other individuals seem to have agreed upon these points: "He is one of the most skillful managers of suits, and has a peculiar faculty in pumping the truth out of a witness . . . He is an excellent reasoner, but his great power lies in his appeals to the feelings of a jury . . ."

One sidelight which seems to have been omitted by others is that, according to Bartlett, "He also has a powerful command of sarcasm, and uses it with great effect occasionally, though it is entirely foreign to his nature to treat any one with severity."

3

Bartlett puts to rest the assumption that Franklin Pierce somehow financed the Willard Williams house on South Main Street in Concord after the Montgomery Street residence (now relocated as the Pierce Manse) was sold on the General's return from the Mexican War.

"General Pierce has no home at present (1852), as, with his wife and child, he boards at a private house in the southern part of the village."

Other authors have maintained that Mrs. Pierce's melancholy nature was instigated by the tragic death of her son Benjamin (in the year following publication of this book). Bartlett indicates, however, that sadness was almost her normal characteristic, the result not only of illness and grief but a failure to seek the bright side of life: "The death of Frank Robert was a terrible stroke upon her, and she has never completely recovered from it. Ever since, she has been more or less of a pensive, melancholy disposition, exceedingly retired and modest. General Pierce . . . for the sake of his wife has often relinquished the highest honors which were pressed upon him; for her sake he has retired from the highest places to the stillness and quietude of a life in the country."

After Pierce's nomination at the Democratic convention, James Buchanan who had sought the office wrote a letter in praise of Pierce, giving rise to the speculation that the latter may have indicated he would support the Pennsylvanian four years later in his bid for the Presidency. The correspondence also deftly sums up Pierce's early political career in one paragraph:

"General Pierce first entered the Senate of the United States on the 4th of March, 1837, and continued to be a member, until the 28th day of February, 1842, when he resigned. This period embraces the whole of Mr. Van Buren's administration and the first year of that of Gen. Harrison and Mr. Tyler. He had previously served as a member of the House of Representatives from December, 1833, until the 4th of March, 1837, throughout General Jackson's second term of office." The author publishes the praise from men as different as Stephen A. Douglas and Sam Houston. The book ends with a statement which was one of the first to be disputed by his enemies as Pierce's four years in office began: "There are few men in the country who have the administrative ability of General Pierce; there are few men who have his firmness of purpose."

Pierce was still President when Charles A. Goodrich had his "History of the United States of America" published by Hickling, Swan & Brown in 1855. However, the copyright date is 1852 and Pierce had not yet been elected. The Mexican War was the most recent event of importance and is treated in considerable detail. Brigadier-General Pierce had not sufficiently distinguished himself to be included in the work. Once nominated for the Presidency, Pierce's war record was an important issue for opposing parties.

"The Presidents of the United States from Washington to Pierce" reached the public soon after the latter completed his administration. The volume was written by John Frost and published by Phillips, Sampson and Company in Boston in 1858 though the manuscript ends with the early days of Pierce's administration. Here are the last paragraphs of the book:

"On the 4th of March 1853, Franklin Pierce was inaugurated President of the United States. His address contained a plain avowal of his political principles, which were those of a large majority of the Democratic party. A love of the Union was conspicuous in this inaugural declaration.

"The cabinet of the new President was formed as follows: William L. Marcy, of New York, Secretary of State; Robert M'Clelland, of Michigan, Secretary of the Interior; James Guthrie, of Kentucky, Secretary of the Treasury; Jefferson Davis, of Mississippi, Secretary of War; James Dobbins, of North Carolina, Secretary of the Navy; Caleb Cushing, of Massachusetts, Attorney-General; and James Campbell, of Pennsylvania, Postmaster-General. The administration of President Pierce began under the brightest auspices, having the support and confidence of a powerful party.

"By an accident on a railroad in Massachusetts, soon after the presidential election, Mr. Pierce lost his only son. He is childless. His wife and his country are all that remain to him demanding his care. Should his future fortune be as bright as his past career, he will furnish an example to young Americans, as one who obtained the highest honors his country could bestow, without resorting to partisan tricks, or mean subterfuge - - as one whom office sought because it found him worthy."

The edition we own was rebound by the Sisters of the Holy Cross who have occupied the estate of Daniel Webster in Franklin, N.H. which he called The Elms. We mention this point because it is extraordinary that while Pierce and Webster were of opposing parties, they espoused some of the same causes.

Webster died a statesman and Pierce a recluse. The President, by the way, was one of the first politicians to seek the Catholic vote and in Concord had long endeared himself to the Irish immigrants who had few persons of native stock to speak up for them.

Horace Greeley like Franklin Pierce was a New Hampshire product, having been born in the same town where Pierce courted Jane Appleton. But Greeley's view of the Civil War was quite at variance with Pierce's. As might be expected, therefore, Greeley treated his fellow Granite Stater as something of a traitor.

In his monumental two-volume work, "The American Conflict," Greeley quotes a speech which Pierce delivered in Concord during the war. The New York publisher concludes: "It can not, surely, be needful to demonstrate that the author of this oration did not regard the Rebel power as **his** enemy, nor that of the country."

Such was Greeley's attitude in the second volume while in the first book he considered Pierce without malice. The

7

tolerance shown towards Pierce's administration may have been due to that section's having been written at a time when animosity toward persons of a more peaceful persuasion had not yet intensified.

"The Court Circles of the Republic" with a subtitle taking up half a page was put out by a conglomerate of publishers in 1870 as a book to be peddled house-to-farm with its appeal in revelations about the famous in Washington. Hartford Publishing Company headed the list of seven companies engaged in the project.

This book by Mrs. E.F. Ellet is dedicated to Mrs. Levi Woodbury, widow of a Governor and Senator from New Hampshire to whom Pierce had been a protegé and eventually a political competitor. "Governor Woodbury was elected Senator in Congress, and a large part of his time was thenceforward necessarily spent in Washington. Mrs. Woodbury accompanied him, and entered metropolitan society. It was then the usage for members of Congress who were agreeable to each other, to form themselves and families into 'messes,' having a table in the boarding-house, or hotel where they lived."

It was in Washington that Pierce became accustomed to the lifestyle of the "mess," influencing his years in Concord where he accepted boarding with a family rather than insisting on his own home as might befit a man of prominence.

Mrs. Ellet's book seems to have the secondary design of promoting the social position of the Woodburys and other friends, most of them probably sources for much of the gossip in the book. However, there are many interesting observations which throw a different light on the Pierce administration. In particular, Mrs. Ellet takes exception to the view that there was very little social life in the White House and that Mrs. Pierce played almost no part in these official affairs. Mrs. Ellet wrote:

"While residing in the executive mansion, Mrs. Pierce never made her own sorrows a reason for any change in the accustomed routine of public affairs, social or official. Although, of course, with no heart for such things during the early portion of the administration of her husband, she considered it her duty to do everything in that regard, which had been done before, or which her social position required.

"For years the established routine of the White House had been a morning reception and an evening reception each week during the session of Congress. These were never intermitted, and Mrs. Pierce invariably 'received' with her husband, unless too ill; often when few could have borne up against her physical suffering. In addition, during the session, General and Mrs. Pierce gave every week a state dinner to which thirty-six persons were invited. Besides, there was rarely a week-day that they dined alone; the guests averaging from three to twelve. Indeed, 'public gaiety' at the White House from 1853 to 1857, was never better known."

This is quite opposite the view of biographers who were not as close to the social amenities as they were to governmental activities. Since apparently Mrs. Ellet was a participant in the events of drawing room and dining room, we have no reason to doubt the truth of what she wrote. The author hints at a reason for the discrepancy:

"Superficial persons who attended the receptions at the White House might mistake the unrivalled grace, dignity and sweetness of Mrs. Pierce's manner, for the result of her great sorrow. But they were in error. The absence of anything like bustle or hurry, and the presence always of repose and gentleness in her bearing, were things innate and inbred, without which she would not have been the lady of refinement she was."

The Civil War was fresh in memory when William

Swinton and the firm of Ivison, Blakeman, Taylor & Co. brought out "A Condensed School History of the United States" in 1871. The author found a good way to deal with Franklin Pierce - - by omitting his name entirely. Whether sentencing him to obscurity was intentional or in the interest of brevity we can't be sure. But Civil War passions were still so heated as to make persona non grata a President who ended his days regretting that the Union had been torn asunder.

"The Centennial History of the United States" - - a volume sold by agents of the National Publishing Company throughout the country in 1875 without credit to its author or more likely its authors - - was probably read by thousands of farm families that had never seen a book store. They did not learn much about Pierce but were told that the Kansas-Nebraska struggle wasn't as one-sided as they had been led to believe.

"The people of the New England States were very anxious that the Indian reservations which covered the eastern part should be bought up by the general government and the country thrown open to emigration. Petitions to this effect were presented to the Thirty-second Congress, but no action was taken upon them until December, 1852, when Mr. Hall, of Missouri, introduced a bill into the House to organize the Territory of Platte."

It is to be noted that while Pierce had been elected he had not yet taken office. The book continues:

"It was referred to the Committee on Territories, which in February, 1853 reported a bill organizing the Territory of Nebraska."

The fat was in the fire before Pierce took office in March. As the volume points out, it was "Senator Douglas, of Illinois, chairman of the Committee on Territories, on the 23d of January, 1854" who "reported a bill which provided for the organization of the Platte country into

10

two Territories." One of the territories, of course, was Kansas and the other Nebraska. Pierce went along with the plan only because it provided that "all questions pertaining to slavery in the Territories, and in the new States to be formed therefrom, are to be left to the decision of the people residing therein, through their appropriate representatives."

It seemed to be a fair solution, and Pierce felt that he was not only recognizing the South but the demands of the North, which had organized settlers to move into the region. The Northern Emigrant Aid Societies first settled at a point on the Kaw River in Kansas and began to build a town which they called Lawrence, in honor of Amos A. Lawrence of Boston, kin of Pierce's wife. On May 21, 1856, the town was burned by a pro-slavery mob.

How this affected Mrs. Pierce we can only imagine but we do know that the President, with an unappreciated attempt at justice, kept replacing governors in the belief that such a move would solve the problem. Pierce acted, and he reminds one of Lincoln replacing generals. Bending over backwards failed just as Pierce's Cabinet representing all factions had not achieved its purpose even though it stayed together throughout the administration.

In 1876, the centennial year, "Lives of the Presidents" with John S.C. Abbott as author, came out under the B.B. Russell imprint from Philadelphia. This book was sold by peddlers and doubtless had a good sale during the exposition of that year.

"When sixteen years of age, in the year 1820, he entered Bowdoin College, at Brunswick, Me.," wrote Pierce's contemporary. "The writer there became personally acquainted with him. He was one of the most popular young men in college. There was something very peculiarly winning in his address, and it was evidently not in the slightest degree studied: it was the simple outgushing of his own magnan-

11

imous and loving nature."

The author gives most of his attention to Pierce's participation in the Mexican War. Ending his chapter, Mr. Abbott shows his own Union bias as follows:

"When the terrible Rebellion burst forth, which divided our country into two parties, and two only, Mr. Pierce remained steadfast in the principles which he had always cherished, and gave his sympathies to that proslavery party with which he had ever been allied. He declined to do anything, either by voice or pen, to strengthen the hands of the National Government. He continued to reside in Concord until the time of his death, which occurred in October, 1869.

"He was one of the most genial and social of men, an honored communicant of the Episcopal Church, and one of the kindest of neighbors. Generous to a fault, he contributed liberally of his moderate means for the alleviation of suffering and want, and many of his townspeople were often gladdened by his material bounty."

"American History for Schools" came not long after the Civil War. Published in 1879 by D. Appleton and Company, it was written by G.P. Quackenbos.

Few pages are devoted to Pierce, and the author skirts any judgment of his administration. Under Foreign Relations, Quackenbos writes:

"Several important questions arose with foreign nations during this administration. First came a boundary dispute with Mexico, which was settled by the Gadsden purchase. . . Next, a sharp discussion took place with Austria as to the right of that country to seize, in a neutral port, one of her subjects who had taken part in the Hungarian Revolution, but had subsequently declared his intention of becoming an American citizen. The position taken by the United States, that the seizure was unlawful, was established, and the Hungarian in question was given up.

"The opening of Japan, before shut out from commercial relations with the rest of the world by its jealousy of foreigners, was effected in 1854. A squadron under Commodore Perry, a brother of the hero of Lake Erie, having visited the Japanese waters, the emperor was induced to sign a treaty by which Americans were allowed to trade at certain ports."

III

Mrs. Jessie Benton Fremont, daughter of a distinguished U.S. Senator and wife of the first Republican candidate for the Presidency, wrote a series of articles called "Souvenirs of My Time" which appeared in a Chautauqua annual that came out in 1886, published by D. Lothrop and Company of Boston.

Though she and her husband were social and political leaders of the opposing party, Mrs. Fremont wrote only in praise of President Pierce. She recounts his offer to have her father live at the White House after the fire which destroyed Senator Benton's home including an extensive library and his manuscripts. "The President came in," she wrote, "too moved to be able to speak at first. He could only grasp my father's hands and choke back his emotion. He had known well what our home was - - what my mother had been in it - - what a friend she had been to him in one turning point in his life."

Most of Mrs. Fremont's reminiscences concern the first ladies. She describes Mrs. Pierce, on coming to the White House, as "already broken in health and now heart-broken."

"Fate . . . took all the life out of her life immediately after the election of President Pierce; their only child, a boy of twelve, was killed - - shockingly mutilated - - in a railroad accident, she beside him, seeing it, but powerless to help. Her woebegone face with its sunken dark eyes, and skin like yellowed ivory, banished all animation in others. She tried but constantly broke down in her efforts to lift, but her life was over, in fact, from the time of that dreadful shock.

"Mr. Pierce, too, felt their loss deeply, but his was a more genial nature. He was a most amiable man whose friends remained always attached to him. He often received alone, and many a pleasant gay circle gathered near the fireplace in the oval room and kept him amused.

"Years before when he had been in the Senate he was much at our house and now he treated me as the child of old friends; although my father had refused personal intercourse with him from some political offense. Coming back as I did from a long absence both in California and then in Europe, Mr. Pierce propitiated my father by coming at once to call on me. Of course my father received him well in his own house and he made me go to the President's, 'for,' he said, 'it is Pierce's head that is wrong - - his heart is always right.' It was indeed . . ."

Textbooks of the past century had little difference in title, and this holds true of "A History of the United States and Its People" written by Edward Eggleston for D. Appleton and Company in 1890.

Eggleston writes off Franklin Pierce very quickly. "He was a man of correct life but of mediocre ability," he notes. The author does bring out an interesting point about Pierce's old crony turned foe: "The little Free-Soil party, which had helped to defeat the Democrats in 1848, cast fewer votes in 1852 for its candidate, John P. Hale, than it had cast for Van Buren in 1848."

While John Sherman did not write a history of the era, his "Recollections of Forty Years in the House, Senate and Cabinet" does throw some light on the Pierce administration as seen by a leading Whig who was not an ardent Abolitionist. The work published by the Werner Company in 1895 contains this appraisal:

"The feeling against the President was embittered by the firm stand taken by him in support of a policy which we regarded as unpatriotic and dangerous in the highest degree to the public peace and the national Union. In his last message he defended or excused the lawless efforts

15

made by residents of Missouri to establish slavery in Kansas. He made no effort to prevent the invasion of Kansas or the crimes committed against its citizens. He appointed many governors for this territory, and in every instance where they sought to protect the rights of its people, he either removed them or denied them his support."

Of course, a member of Pierce's Democratic party might well have asked: "What could President Pierce have done without ordering military intervention as commander-in-chief; and if armed force in great numbers was ordered to march, how could its neutrality be assured and how could a buildup to national conflict have been prevented?"

Sherman does present a sidelight not found elsewhere: "The political excitement existing during the whole of President Pierce's term entered into social life in Washington. The President was not brought into contact with those who differed with him in opinion. His family afflictions were, no doubt, the partial cause of this. The sincere friendship that often exists between political adversaries in public life (was) not possible during this period. Social lines were drawn on sectional lines, and in the north, party lines became hostile lines.

"Such causes, no doubt, led to unjust criticism of the President, and, in turn, caused him to regard his political adversaries as enemies to their country and disturbers of the public peace. I scarcely remember seeing him during this Congress and was strongly prejudiced against him. A more careful study of the motives and conduct of public men during this period has changed my opinion of many of them, and, especially, of President Pierce. That he was a genial, social and agreeable companion is affirmed by all who were familiar with him. That his opinions were honestly entertained, and firmly supported, is shown by his adherence to them without change or shadow of turning.

In this respect he compares favorably with many leading men of his party, who stifled their opinions to meet the current of the day. He had been a general of distinction in the Mexican War and a member of both the Senate and House of Representatives. He was a leading lawyer in his state. His messages to Congress, considered in a literary view, were able state papers, clearly and strongly expressed. It was his great misfortune to have to deal with a controversy that he did not commence, but he did not shrink from the responsibility. He believed in the policy of non-intervention in the territories and so did not prevent the 'border ruffians' of Missouri crossing the line and voting at every election in Kansas, setting up a bogus Legislature, adopting the laws of Missouri as the laws of Kansas, and establishing negro slavery in that territory.

"With the kindly biography of President Pierce, written by his friend, Nathaniel Hawthorne, before me, I can appreciate his ability, integrity and agreeable social qualities, and only regret that he was President of the United States at a time when the sagacity of a Jefferson, the determined courage of a Jackson, or the shrewdness and wisdom of a Lincoln, were needed to meet the difficulties and dangers which he had to encounter."

These views of a future Secretary of State may be representative of opinions held by Pierce's Whig opponents who did not subscribe to the more vitriolic attacks of the Abolitionist stripe.

Another eventual Secretary of State who was on the Republican side of the fence was James G. Blaine who wrote "Twenty Years of Congress", and these reminiscences were published by The Henry Bill Publishing Company in 1884. The unsuccessful candidate for President points out how rosy a picture faced the Democrats after Pierce's election:

"The Democratic party, seeing their old Whig rival prostrate, naturally concluded that a long lease of power was granted them. The victory of Pierce was so complete that his supporters could not with closest scrutiny descry an opponent worthy of the slightest consideration. The Democrats . . . beheld the country prosperous in all its material interests, and they saw the mass of the people content in both sections with settlement of the slavery question. There was no national disquietude on the vexed question of slavery when Franklin Pierce was installed as President."

IV

In 1897, classes began to read "The Student's American History" by D.H. Montgomery and published by Ginn and Company. The book has little to say about Pierce, quoting the inaugural address and then stating that the slavery question was kept in the background "for a brief period while America took part in an international exhibition." This was the first World's Fair, held in 1853 in New York's Crystal Palace. "The foreign department was noted for its large and valuable collection of works of art. The American department took the front rank in the variety of its woodworking machinery and agricultural implements."

This observation that Europe was more interested in the arts and the United States overwhelmingly committed to mechanical progress is a point that should be underscored.

Practically the next mention of Pierce is in the summary where Montgomery concludes: "The principal events of Pierce's administration were: (1) the passage of the Kansas-Nebraska Act, repealing the Missouri Compromise and applying the principle of Popular Sovereignty to the settlement of the question of slavery extension in those territories; (2) the struggle between the North and the South for the possession of Kansas; (3) the rise of the Republican party; (4) the opening of the first American World's Fair, the treaty with Japan, the attempts of the government to purchase Cuba, and the Ostend Manifesto."

While these events happened during Pierce's administration, they do not constitute a summary of his accomplishments. This historical perspective is one which we call downgrading by overlooking. Much could have been said in Pierce's favor which was omitted.

Also in 1897, "The Presidents of the United States"

written by Henry W. Rugg, D.D., was published by J.A. and R.A. Reid in Boston.

In a compilation of such scope, the author must usually rely on a few secondary sources for each chapter, so we cannot expect to find much that is new in the sketch of Pierce. We are told that "He achieved wonderful success as a lawyer, his popularity doubtless depending not only upon the mental powers and intellectual training which he displayed, but also upon his gracious, urbane manners; his great personal magnetism influencing juries as it influenced all his associates. Never was a man more courteous in his treatment of friends and foes; he was always calm, moderate, and even-tempered, however trying the occasion or vexatious the circumstances."

This encomium is enlarged upon in the final summary: "One of President Pierce's distinguishing characteristics was the steadfastness which he showed in his friendships. He attached himself very deeply to those whom he thought merited his confidence, believing in them so strongly that he was willing to hear no criticism of their actions from others, though perhaps he admitted to himself that it was deserved.

"The cheerful, social qualities of this representative man were best shown in his personal life, where he delighted in the meeting of congenial acquaintances and exercised a most cordial hospitality. There was something attractive in his bearing which caused even strangers to feel the warmth of his personality and be induced to linger in his presence . . . Men liked to hear his words upon any subject, and unconsciously were influenced by that charm which pervaded his being. These amiable graces which he exercised were more powerful to win for him success, than more striking qualities of greatness would have been; they appealed directly to the hearts of men, and did not shock them, as genius sometimes does, into a forced appreciation

20

of its greatness. While not underrating President Pierce's intellectual abilities, it may be justly said that in his human sympathies, his warm heart, his courteous demeanor, was hidden the secret of his success in life; the sweetness of disposition which entered into his manly, upright nature, would have made him a noticeable character, even had he not been exalted to the high rank of a political leader, and called upon to assume the helm of national affairs."

Books for public schools over-simplified most of history, as might be expected, and this is true of "The Story of the Great Republic" by A.A. Guerber which the American Book Company put out in 1899.

"Pierce had been a poor lad," says the author, with some slight twisting of the truth, "but he managed to secure a good education. He then became a lawyer and was so determined to succeed that when some people made fun of him, after a first failure, he firmly said: 'I will try 999 cases, if clients continue to trust me; and if I fail just as I have failed today, I will try the thousandth. I shall live to argue cases in this courthouse in a manner that will mortify neither myself nor my friends.' As the young man proved as good as his word, it will not surprise you to hear that he did succeed."

Guerber points out that "it was not in Pierce's power to put an end to the quarrel of those who were for or against slavery, although he made a good President . . . It was under Pierce, too, that our fleet came home from Japan where a treaty was made which allowed our ships to trade there. Ever since then, America has kept up a lively trade with Japan, where the people are learning civilized ways so rapidly that it is said they will soon overtake the most advanced countries."

V

Interesting glimpses of Pierce are given by Henry McFarland who had "Sixty Years in Concord" privately printed in 1899. As a youth, he was a clerk in the Franklin Bookstore where was displayed the sword presented to the brigadier general by the Legislature in 1849. The author adds: "The general received a similar weapon from ladies of Concord in May 1847 and the presentation speech was made by the daughter of a clergyman whose son, a soldier, was afterward tried for murder in a Western state."

"Gen. Franklin Pierce came in rather often" to the bookstore, McFarland wrote, adding a revelation that "a scheme to effect his nomination" as President was hatched as early as his return from the Mexican War. Those planning the strategy are named as Pierre Soulé, Edmund Ruffin, John S. Barbour and "probably" Jefferson Davis.

McFarland wrote that in July 1860, when he was a newspaperman, "General Pierce, General Peaslee, and other prominent Democrats found it convenient to be out of town" the day Stephen A. Douglas visited Concord. Douglas "was then out of favor" with Pierce's branch of the Democratic party.

The author quotes Judge Asa Fowler, Pierce's old partner, as saying he was satisfied in February 1861 there would be no war. The New Hampshire Statesman, however, printed this paragraph: "We hear that ex-President Pierce, whose sources of information are said to be of the most fortunate character, regards a dissolution of the Union as inevitable." McFarland adds that when Douglas was in Concord he said privately that "Lincoln would be elected and war would follow."

McFarland apparently was one of those Concord citizens who heard Pierce speak on April 16, 1861, from the balcony of the Eagle Hotel, the Main Street inn that he had backed with his money years before. (A settee used by Pierce from this hotel is displayed in the restored Pierce Manse.)

"The address, spoken as it was with earnestness of manner, sounded well, and was received with cheers, but there is not much battle smoke in it," wrote McFarland. What he apparently meant was that while Pierce was urging his audience to stand together and "uphold the flag to the last," the ex-President was not encouraging the people of Concord to take up arms.

The last mention of Pierce in the book relates to the letter which Pierce sent to Jefferson Davis the year before. Pierce had written that if the Abolitionists through their madness instigated a war, fighting would erupt in the North as well as the South. When the letter came to light in 1863 through the looting of the Davis plantation in Mississippi, most Northerners took this to mean that Pierce was promising the South armed support should hostilities commence. To us this seems a gross misreading of the letter from one old friend to another. It meant, in our opinion, only that fighting was likely to spread above "Mason and Dixon's line" once started in the South and that it was thus important not to let hostilities erupt anywhere in the nation.

But with publication of the letter, Pierce was ostracized by the people of Concord and considered a traitor by many. The war fever was raging, and no temperate view was tenable.

It took many years for the New Hampshire Legislature to approve a statue of President Pierce just outside the sacred bounds of the State House yard. Almost a full century following his death was required to interest Concord in saving his family home from demolition. Now that the Pierce Manse has been restored in the capital city's historic district, the nation is taking a fresh look at the life of the 14th U.S. President.

Would the Civil War have occurred if he had been elected eight years later? Could Pierce have ended slavery, which he deplored, by compensatory rather than violent means?

We shall never have the answers. We do feel that Franklin Pierce was a Presidential martyr - - not through war nor treachery but because of character assassination by elements spoiling for battle, heedless of a statesman who was for all the states and not one section alone.

In the Pierce Manse at the far end of North Main Street in Concord, overlooking Horseshoe Pond, visitors can see how the man who was to become President lived with his family before the Mexican War. These rooms not only contain many of the furnishings used by the then Col. Pierce, his wife and two children but also those walls enclose the pleasures and worries, the hopes and failures, of a man who under different circumstances might have kept the country on his side, true to the principle that the United States could stay united only by respecting the rights of each state.